WEATHER

Chris Oxlade

an imprint of Hodder Children's Books

SCIENCE FACT FILES

THE EARTH'S RESOURCES
ELECTRICITY AND MAGNETISM
FORCES AND MOTION
LIGHT AND SOUND
THE SOLAR SYSTEM
WEATHER

Produced by Roger Coote Publishing
Gissing's Farm, Fressingfield
Suffolk IP21 5SH

First published in 2000 by Hodder Wayland
An imprint of Hodder Children's Books
This paperback edition published in 2001
Text copyright © 2000 Hodder Wayland
Volume copyright © 2000 Hodder Wayland

Design and typesetting Victoria Webb
Commissioning Editor Lisa Edwards
Editor Sarah Doughty
Picture Researcher Lynda Lines
Illustrator Alex Pang

Endpaper picture: A tornado in the USA
Title page picture: Lightning

We are grateful to the following for permission to reproduce photographs:
Camera Press 27 (Keystone), 35; Corbis *front endpapers*; Digital Stock 33 bottom, 41 top; Digital Vision *front cover bottom right*, 5, 23, 25, 42; MPM Images 8, 12 top, 14, 15 top, 19, 24, 31, 33 top, 40 left, 40 right, 41 bottom; Science Photo Library *front cover background* (NASA) *and top right* (Scott Camazine), 10 (Sam Ogden), 11 (Damien Lovegrove), 12 bottom (Jerome Yeats), 15 bottom (Magrath/Folsom), 16 (Peter Menzel), 17 top, 17 bottom (NCAR), 18 (Simon Fraser), 21 (Stephen Krasemann), 22 (Pekka Parviainen), 28 (University of Dundee), 32 (Simon Fraser), 34 (NASA), 36 (Simon Fraser), 37 left (Tony Buxton), 37 right (David Parker), 38 (Hank Morgan), 43 (DA Peel).

The statistics given in this book are the most up to date available at the time of going to press.

Printed in Hong Kong by Wing King Tong

A CIP catalogue record for this book is available from the British Library
ISBN 0 7500 2721 5

Hodder Children's Books
A division of Hodder Headline Limited
338 Euston Road, London NW1 3BH

CONTENTS

The words that are explained in the glossary are printed
in **bold** the first time they are mentioned in the text.

INTRODUCTION

The weather is an important part of our everyday lives. It dictates what clothes we wear and where we go on holiday. But it is much more important for people such as fishermen and pilots, who try to avoid bad weather for safety reasons. In some parts of the world, hurricanes, floods and other weather disasters are a regular hazard.

The science of the weather is called meteorology, and people who study it are called meteorologists. This book starts by looking at why weather phenomena such as clouds, winds and rain happen, and at weather patterns such as the seasons. Then it describes how the weather affects our lives, and how weather forecasts are made. Finally, it explains how our activities may be making the world's weather change.

The Atmosphere

The Earth is surrounded by a layer of air called the atmosphere. Weather happens as the air in the part of the atmosphere nearest the Earth's surface swirls about. If you could travel straight upwards from the Earth's surface, you would find that the **density** of the air gets less and less. The atmosphere has no definite edge, but you can think of space starting about 200 km up from the Earth's surface. This is where spacecraft such as the space shuttle orbit the Earth. The atmosphere is very thin compared to the size if the Earth – it's a bit like the skin on an apple. The air that makes up the atmosphere is a mixture of gases, but is mostly nitrogen and oxygen, the gas that we need to breathe. There is also a small amount of water vapour in the air.

In this view of Earth from space, the continents are partly obscured by clouds in the lower atmosphere.

This pie chart shows the percentage of different gases that make up the Earth's atmosphere. Air often contains up to 4 per cent water vapour as well. The more water vapour there is, the less nitrogen and oxygen.

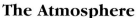

Oxygen 21%

Other gases – total of 1% (mostly argon, but also a tiny amount of carbon dioxide)

Nitrogen 78%

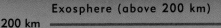

Exosphere (above 200 km)

200 km ——————————————

FACT FILE

ALTITUDE DATA
• Three-quarters of all the air in the atmosphere is contained in the troposphere.
• As **altitude** increases, air temperature falls in the troposphere, rises in the stratosphere, falls again in the mesosphere, and rises again in the thermosphere.
• The air temperature at the top of the thermosphere can reach more than 1,500 °C.
• At sea level, each litre of air contains about 25,000 million million million **molecules** of gas.

Thermosphere (80–200 km)

80 km ——————————————

Mesosphere (50–80 km)

50 km ——————————————

The layers of
the Earth's
atmosphere

Stratosphere (10–50 km)

10 km ——————————————

Troposphere (up to an average of 10 km)

Sea level

Layers of the Atmosphere

Meteorologists divide the atmosphere into several layers. Each layer has its own variations of air temperature and mixture of gases. Most weather happens in the bottom layer, called the troposphere.

The air temperature in the troposphere reduces with altitude by about 7 °C per km. It stops changing at the top of the troposphere, which is called the tropopause, where the temperature is about −60 °C.

MEASURING THE ATMOSPHERE

Weather phenomena such as rain and wind are created by the temperature, pressure and **humidity** of the air. To understand how the weather works (and so to forecast it), meteorologists need to understand these properties and how to measure them.

Temperature

Temperature is a measure of how hot something is. Heat, which is a form of energy, always flows from hotter things to cooler things. Meteorologists measure temperature in degrees Celsius (°C) or degrees Fahrenheit (°F) using a thermometer. Liquid-in-glass thermometers contain liquid which expands along a very narrow tube as the temperature rises. Digital thermometers measure the temperature electronically. A specialist meteorological thermometer is the maximum and minimum thermometer, which records the highest and lowest temperatures over a period of time.

Pressure

Pressure is the amount of force pressing on a certain area. The unit of pressure is the pascal. The pressure created by the air in the atmosphere is called atmospheric pressure. On the Earth's surface, atmospheric pressure is about 10 million pascals or 1,000 hectopascals (or millibars).

Air pressure is measured with a barometer. The most common type is the aneroid barometer. This has a metal container with air pumped out, creating a vacuum inside. As the air pressure changes, the box changes size slightly, making a pointer move on a scale. In a column barometer, air pressure pushes liquid (normally mercury) up a glass column. As the air pressure rises, the level of liquid rises. This is why pressure is sometimes stated in millimetres of mercury rather than hectopascals.

This barometer measures air pressure and displays it as a line on a graph.

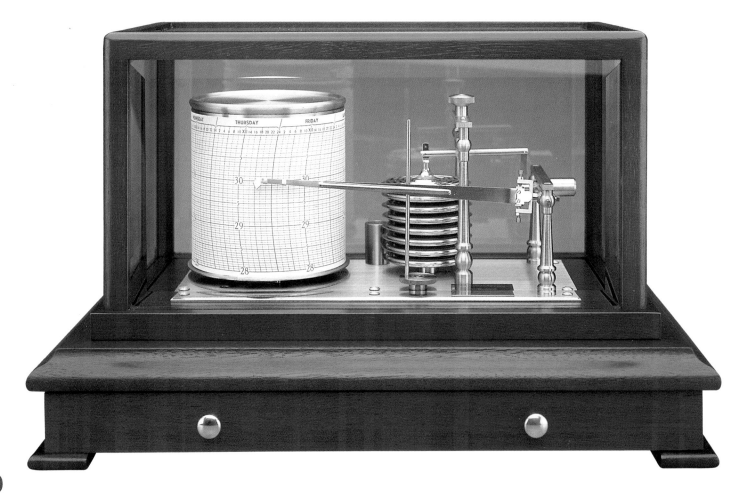

HISTORY FILE

THE COLUMN BAROMETER

Evangelista Torricelli (1608–1647) was an Italian scientist and mathematician. In one of his experiments, he filled a long glass tube with mercury and turned it upside down with its open end in a dish, also filled with mercury. Some mercury stayed in the tube, and Torricelli realized that this was because of atmospheric pressure pressing down on the mercury in the dish. Torricelli had invented the column barometer.

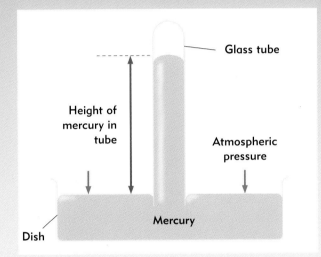

Glass tube

Height of mercury in tube

Atmospheric pressure

Mercury

Dish

A column barometer. The greater the atmospheric pressure, the higher the mercury is pushed up the column.

Humidity

Air always contains some water vapour. It is formed when water molecules escape from the surface of liquid water into the air. This process is called **evaporation**. Air can hold only a certain amount of water vapour until it becomes **saturated**, but warmer air can hold more than colder air. This means that as warm, saturated air cools, some water vapour must turn back into liquid water because the air can no longer hold it all. This is called condensation. The amount of water vapour in the air is called humidity. Meteorologists normally measure **relative humidity**. Dry air has 0 per cent relative humidity; saturated air has 100 per cent relative humidity.

These two thermometers at a weather station are designed to measure relative humidity. The screen behind the thermometers protects them from wind and rain, which would cause them to give false readings.

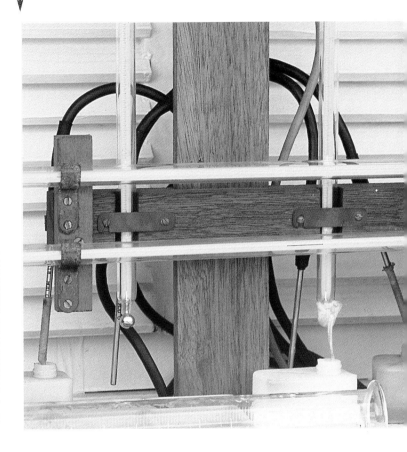

TEST FILE

CONDENSATION

Fill a plastic bottle with warm water, swirl the water about and pour it out, leaving the bottle full of humid air. Now plunge the bottle into cold water. Water droplets appear on the inside of the bottle as some of the water vapour condenses.

DRIVING THE WEATHER

Nothing happens without energy to make it happen – and that includes the weather. The energy that drives the weather comes from the Sun, and it travels through space to the Earth in the form of **radiation**. This radiation is made up of light, heat and other forms of radiation, such as ultraviolet radiation. Heat radiation travels through the atmosphere, hits the land, seas and oceans, and warms them up. This heat then warms the air above the land and water.

The air is heated more in some places than others, and it moves around to try to even out the distribution of heat over the Earth's surface. This happens on a local level, but also on a global level (see page 26). The air also collects and loses water vapour as it moves, creating rain, snow and other forms of **precipitation**.

Rising Air

When air is heated, it expands to take up more space. This makes its density slightly less than the cooler air around it, and it floats upwards, just as an air-filled ball floats upwards in water. In the same way, if air is cooled, it becomes more dense than the warmer air around it and sinks downwards. The currents of moving air created are called **convection** currents.

When water vapour in clouds freezes it forms ice crystals which fall as snow.

Glider, hang-glider and paraglider pilots search out thermals (rising currents of warm air) to keep them airborne.

 TEST FILE

HEAT ABSORPTION
Cut two pieces of card about 10 cm square, one white and one black. Prop the pieces of card up so that their faces point towards the Sun. After ten minutes, feel the pieces of card. The black card will be hotter because it absorbs heat more efficiently than the white card. In the same way, dark-coloured soil and rocks on the Earth's surface heat up more quickly than those that are lighter in colour.

Heating the Ground

The Sun does not heat the Earth's surface evenly. Some types of land, such as bare, dark-coloured soil, absorb much more heat from the Sun than land covered with forest or deep water. They also cool more quickly.

The angle at which the Sun's rays hit the ground also affects the heating of the Earth's surface. The rays are most concentrated when they hit the ground at right angles. If they hit at a shallow angle, they are spread over a wider area, and so are less concentrated. This means that the surface near the **Equator** is heated more than the surface at higher **latitude**s, towards the poles, and that the heating effect is greatest in the middle of the day when the Sun is highest in the sky. The amount of heating also depends on cloud cover because clouds block the path of the Sun's rays to the ground.

FACT FILE

TEMPERATURE DATA
• In hot sunshine, dark-coloured soil and rocks can reach temperatures of more than 80 °C.
• Ground which absorbs heat well in the day loses it quickly at night, too. This means that deserts can be very hot in the day and very cold not long after the Sun sets.
• The oceans stay at the same temperature day and night.
• The Earth receives just less than a thousand millionth of the total energy given out by the Sun.

Around the Equator the Sun's rays are more concentrated on the ground than at the poles.

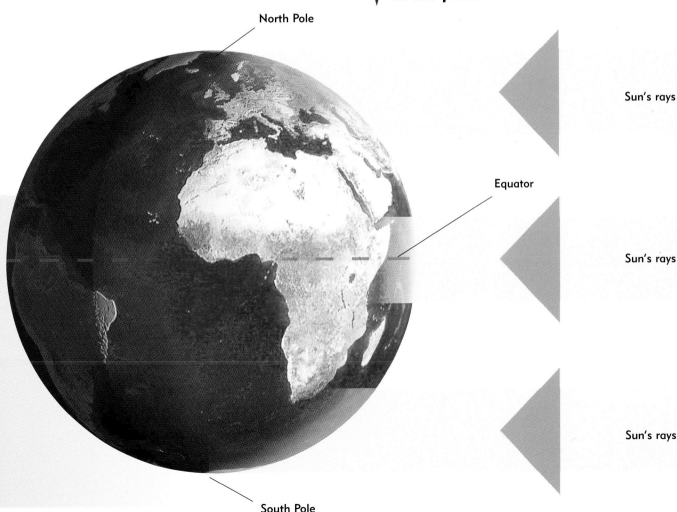

North Pole

Sun's rays

Equator

Sun's rays

Sun's rays

South Pole

CLOUDS

All clouds, whether they are white and fluffy or grey and towering, are made up of millions and millions of particles of water. In low-level clouds the particles are tiny water droplets. Higher up, where the air temperature is below freezing point, they are ice crystals. Some clouds may contain both droplets and crystals.

We can see clouds because sunlight is scattered by their water droplets or ice crystals. Thin clouds look white because they allow most of the Sun's rays to pass through them. Thicker clouds look grey because most sunlight is reflected back into the sky.

Cloud Formation

When air cools, the amount of water vapour it can hold decreases. So if air that contains water vapour cools enough, some of the vapour condenses, forming droplets of water. If the temperature is below freezing, the water vapour turns straight into ice crystals.

Air normally cools because it rises up through the atmosphere. If it cools enough, water vapour in it condenses to form clouds. There are three common ways in which air rises. Firstly, it can be heated by warm ground and bubble upwards, forming rising air currents called **thermals**. Secondly, it can be pushed upwards as it blows into mountains. Finally, it can rise over colder air in a front (see page 28). Air can also be cooled if it passes over cool ground or water (see page 18).

Cloud formed when air rises over mountains is called orographic cloud.

Cloud

Water vapour condenses to form cloud

Warm air rising

Warm air rising

On a warm day, air heated by the ground rises to create clouds.

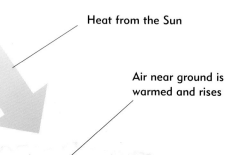

Heat from the Sun

Air near ground is warmed and rises

Cloud Types

There are many different types of cloud and names for them, but there are only two basic forms – puffy, heaped clouds called cumuliform (which are normally formed by thermals and on mountains) and flat, layered clouds called stratiform (which are normally created in fronts).

Cloud names also describe the clouds' altitude. High-level clouds (those above 5,000 m) are called cirrus or have names starting with 'cirro'. Mid-level clouds (those between 2,000 m and 5,000 m) have names starting with 'alto'. Low-level clouds (those below 2,000 m) have no prefix.

Most cloud names are a combination of cloud type and altitude. For example, 'altostratus' clouds are mid-level ('alto') layered ('stratus') clouds.

HISTORY FILE

CLOUD CLASSIFICATION

The person who devised the classification of clouds that we use today was English scientist Luke Howard (1772–1864). At the time, Latin was the language of science, and Howard simply used the Latin words which best described the shape of the clouds. For example, cumulus means 'heap', stratus means 'layer' and cirrus means 'curl of hair'. (See the endpaper at the back of the book for more information.)

Main picture: Fluffy cumulus clouds. Their bases are black because light cannot get through from above.

Inset: Lenticular clouds are a type of altocumulus cloud that often form over mountains. They are sometimes mistaken for flying saucers.

RAIN, SNOW AND HAIL

Any water that falls from the sky is called precipitation. It can be in the form of rain, snow or hail. The water droplets or ice crystals that make up clouds are very tiny indeed, measuring no more than a hundredth of a millimetre across. Because they are so small, they swirl about in the air currents inside the cloud rather than falling to the ground.

But when water droplets or ice crystals grow into larger droplets, they become heavy enough to fall from the cloud. In low-level clouds, this happens when water droplets collide to form larger droplets. This process is called coalescence. In high-level clouds, ice crystals grow larger and larger as molecules of water vapour join them.

Floods happen when rivers burst their banks after rain falls steadily for days on end. Even more destructive are flash floods, caused by very heavy rain falling on ground that is already saturated.

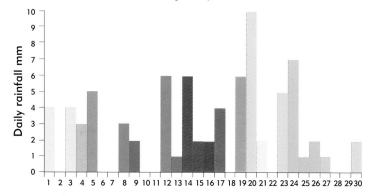

Rainfall is normally shown on a bar graph. These graphs show daily rainfall over a month and average monthly rainfall over a year for Hong Kong.

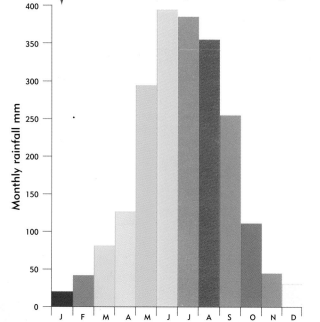

FACT FILE

WEATHER RECORDS
• The place with the highest recorded average annual rainfall in the world is Mawsynram in India, with 11,875 mm.
• The place with the lowest recorded average annual rainfall in the world is the Atacama Desert in Chile, with 0.08 mm.
• Paradise, near Mount Rainier, USA, has the highest recorded annual snowfall, with 31,102 mm.
• The largest hailstone ever measured fell in Bangladesh in 1986 and weighed 1.02 kg.
• In 1982, 92 people were killed in Bangladesh by hailstones weighing up to 1 kg each.

Rainfall is measured in a rain gauge. The water trickles through the funnel into a jar. Each day the rainfall is measured in millimetres by pouring the water into the cylinder.

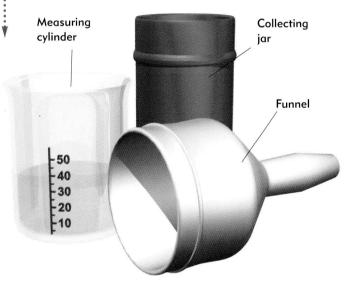

Measuring cylinder

Collecting jar

Funnel

50
40
30
20
10

Rain

Rain drops are either water droplets from low-level clouds, or ice crystals from higher-level clouds which melt as they fall through warm air. Freezing rain is formed when water drops freeze as they fall through cold air after leaving a cloud.

Rain drops can be up to 5 mm across. Very light rain called is called drizzle and is made up of rain drops less than 0.1 mm across. Stratus clouds tend to create long periods of steady rain. Cumulus clouds tend to produce short showers.

Measuring Rainfall

The amount of rain that falls at a place is measured by the depth, normally in millimetres, of the pool of water it would make if it did not drain away or evaporate. The measurement is made with a rain gauge, which is a flat-bottomed container with a funnel-shaped lid to reduce evaporation.

Snow

Snow is made up of large ice crystals which grow inside clouds from much smaller crystals. The growing process creates six-sided crystals with intricate shapes. When it is very cold, snow forms small, dry flakes, making powder snow on the ground. In warmer temperatures, larger, wetter flakes are created. In extremely cold temperatures, it does not tend to snow because the air cannot hold enough water vapour for crystals to form.

Hail is formed in cumulonimbus clouds. Frozen water droplets circulate up and down again and again inside the clouds, growing larger until they are so heavy they fall to the ground.

DEW, FROST AND FOG

When you fill a bath with hot water in a cool bathroom, the bathroom mirror mists up. This is because warm, damp air created above the bath water moves around the bathroom, and hits the cold glass, where the water vapour condenses back to liquid water, forming tiny droplets on the surface. Dew, frost and fog are formed in a similar way, when humid air comes close to cold ground or water.

Dew and Frost

On cold nights when there is little cloud cover, the ground quickly cools as heat escapes into the atmosphere by radiation. Water vapour then condenses on to the ground, plants and other objects, forming dew.

If the ground temperature is below freezing, the water vapour turns straight into ice. A layer of ice crystals, often with intricate flowery patterns, forms on the ground, plants and other objects. This is called frost, or more properly hoar frost. Frost also forms when dew freezes, but this is not hoar frost.

Fog

Fog forms at night when water vapour condenses just above the ground rather than on it. Fog is like very low-level cloud, sometimes just a few metres thick, sometimes hundreds of metres thick.

Radiation fog forms when heat leaves the ground at night by radiation, cooling the air just above the ground. Advection fog forms when warm, humid air drifts across cold ground or water. For example, sea fog forms when humid air from above an area of warm water drifts across an area of colder water.

Fog clears if the Sun heats the ground (and so the air above it) during the day, but if cloud appears at the end of the night, blocking the sunshine, fog can last all day. Fog is normally made worse by pollution in the air because water condenses easily on to particles of soot and dust in polluted air.

Haze and Smog

Haze is a low-level layer of **pollutants** that forms over several days in still, dry weather conditions. It is most likely to form over large industrial cities. Smog is an extreme form of haze created when water vapour condenses on to particles of dust and smoke in the air. The build-up of pollutants is a health hazard to residents and can spoil stone buildings over a long period of time.

Hoar frost coating the branches of trees.

HISTORY FILE

'PEA-SOUPERS'
In the first half of the twentieth century, northern European cities suffered with smogs because people burned large amounts of coal for domestic heating. In London, the smogs were called 'pea-soupers'. They caused thousands of deaths. The smogs were reduced by the introduction of laws restricting the use of smoke-producing fuels.

Smog over New York, USA, formed because of the high level of pollutants from vehicle exhausts.

WIND

Wind is simply moving air. The air moves from areas of high pressure to areas of low pressure to try to equalize the pressure in both areas. Imagine a chunk of air above a hot area of land being heated. The air expands and rises, leaving an area of low pressure. Cooler air flows into the area from around it, where the pressure is higher. This movement is felt as a gentle breeze at ground level.

Sea Breezes

A similar thing happens in coastal areas on hot, still days to create winds called sea breezes. During the day, the land heats up quickly in the sunshine. Hot air rises from the land, creating low pressure, and cooler air comes in from over the sea to equalize the pressure. This creates a cool onshore breeze off the sea.

When the Sun goes down, the land loses heat quickly and becomes colder than the sea. Now the circulation of air reverses, creating an offshore breeze.

FACT FILE

WORLD WINDS
In many parts of the world there are winds which blow from the same direction at the same time each year. Here are some examples:

- **Chinook** – a warm, dry wind which blows east of the Rocky Mountains in the USA.
- **Föhn** – a warm wind which blows down from the Alps in Europe.
- **Harmattan** – a cool, dry easterly wind in north-west Africa which also carries dust from the desert.
- **Levanter** – an easterly wind in the Straits of Gibraltar between Spain and North Africa.
- **Mistral** – a wind which blows southwards through France and into the Mediterranean.
- **Sirocco** – a hot, dry, southerly wind which blows from North Africa across the Mediterranean and into Europe.

Daytime sea breeze

Hot land 18 °C

Sea cooler than land 12 °C

Cool onshore breeze blows from sea to land

Sea still warm 12 °C

Offshore breeze blows from land to sea

Night-time land breeze

Cooled land 8 °C

Stronger winds on a much greater scale are created by the movement of huge chunks of air, called air masses, across the surface of the Earth. Their movement is also caused by areas of high and low pressure. You can find out about air masses on page 26.

Measuring Wind

Wind is described in terms of its speed and direction. Speed is measured in kilometres per hour (kph). The direction of a wind is the compass direction from which the wind blows. For example, a northerly wind comes from the north and blows towards the south.

Wind speed is measured using a device called an anemometer. Most anemometers have cups which are spun by the wind, always in the same direction. The wind direction is detected by a weather vane, which points in the direction that the wind is blowing from. Near the ground, the strength of a wind is decreased by trees and buildings, which also make the wind gusty, so wind speed and direction must be measured at an open site.

Anemometers set up to measure wind speed at different heights above the ground.

TEST FILE

JUDGING WIND SPEED

In the early nineteenth century, Sir Francis Beaufort devised the scale below as a way of estimating the speed of the wind by observing the ways in which it affects things such as smoke rising, trees swaying, and so on. See if you can work out the speed of the wind using the Beaufort Scale.

Force	kph	Description	Observations
0	0	Calm	Smoke rises vertically
1	1–5	Light airs	Smoke drifts slowly
2	6–11	Light breeze	Leaves rustle
3	12–19	Gentle breeze	Leaves and twigs of trees move
4	20–29	Moderate breeze	Small trees move; dust blows about
5	30–38	Fresh breeze	Small trees sway
6	39–51	Strong breeze	Large branches move
7	52–61	Near gale	Large trees sway; walking into wind difficult
8	62–74	Gale	Twigs snap off trees
9	75–86	Severe gale	Roof slates dislodged; branches snap
10	87–101	Storm	Trees uprooted; structural damage
11	102–119	Violent storm	Widespread damage
12	120 +	Hurricane	Widespread destruction

THUNDER AND LIGHTNING

Two of the most spectacular weather phenomena, thunder and lightning, are created by electrical activity inside enormous storm clouds. In fact, thunder and lightning are the same event – thunder is simply the noise created by a lightning strike. Lightning happens when electricity builds up inside a cloud, causing huge sparks to jump within the cloud or from the cloud to the ground. The conditions for thunderstorms are normally warm temperatures and humid air, which is why most thunderstorms happen in the **tropics**.

Inside a Storm Cloud

Thunderclouds are formed when warm, humid air rises quickly, creating strong upward convection currents. If there is a large enough supply of humid air, cumulonimbus clouds form. These clouds can stretch nearly 20,000 m into the sky, and if they reach the top of the troposphere, they spread to create anvil-shaped thunderclouds.

The unmistakable anvil-topped shape of a thunder-making cumulonimbus cloud.

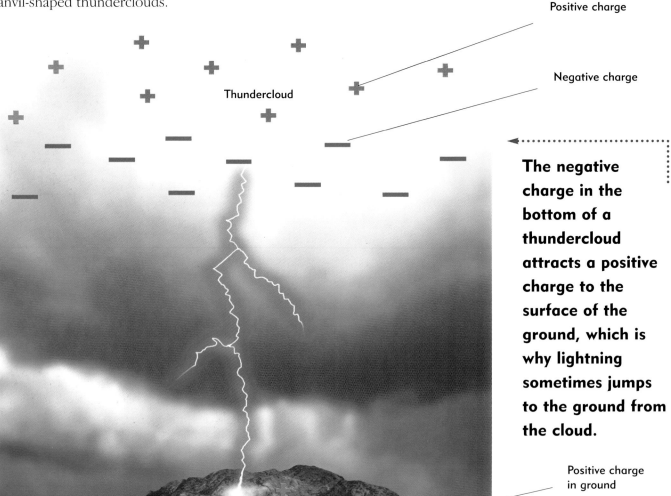

Positive charge

Negative charge

Thundercloud

The negative charge in the bottom of a thundercloud attracts a positive charge to the surface of the ground, which is why lightning sometimes jumps to the ground from the cloud.

Positive charge in ground

FACT FILE

STORM FACTS
• Tall, thin objects, such as church spires, concentrate electrical charges and are more likely to be hit by lightning.
• On average, there are 40,000 thunderstorms every day around the world, and lightning strikes the Earth a hundred times each second.
• Ball lightning is extremely rare. It takes the form of a glowing ball of light drifting through the air.
• The distance to a thunderstorm in kilometres equals the time in seconds between the lightning and thunder divided by three.
• Lightning can strike twice in the same place!

A lightning strike captured on film. Although we see only a brief flash, electricity actually flows up and down several times during the strike

Cooling air also plunges back down through the cloud, creating severe turbulence, which is extremely dangerous to aircraft. The strong currents also create heavy rain and hail. Eventually, the downward currents become stronger than the upward currents, and the storm subsides.

Lightning Strikes

Static electricity is electric charge that builds up on the surface of objects. For example, if you comb your hair with a nylon comb, static electricity builds up on the comb and on your hair. One is a positive charge and the other a negative charge. These two types of charge attract each other, which is why your hair is attracted to the comb.

Inside a storm cloud, strong electric currents cause charges to build up on particles of ice and water inside the cloud. Negative charges build up in the bottom of the cloud and positive charges build up in the top. Eventually, when the charges are high enough, a spark jumps, cancelling out the charges. This is called a lightning discharge. It can happen between the top and bottom of a cloud, between two clouds, or between the cloud and the ground.

Along the path of the lightning, the air is heated very quickly, making it expand. This creates a wave of pressure which moves through the air, and which we hear as rumbling thunder. We hear thunder later than we see lightning because sound travels much more slowly than light.

HISTORY FILE

LIGHTNING TO ELECTRICITY
The first person to make the link between lightning and electricity was American statesman and scientist Benjamin Franklin (1706–90). To prove his theory, he flew a kite on a thin wire during a thunderstorm. Lightning struck the kite and electricity flowed down the wire. Luckily for Franklin, it did not flow through him.

WEATHERING

The weather has a huge effect on the appearance of the Earth's surface. Changes of temperature, rain and winds gradually erode (wear away) the landscape in some places and build it up in others. For example, rain water that flows down rivers creates valleys and washes **sediment** to the sea, building up the sea-bed.

The Water Cycle

A great deal of weathering is caused by the circulation of water between the land and the sea. This circulation is called the water cycle. It happens as water evaporates from the oceans, seas, lakes, soil and plants, is carried as water vapour in the air and eventually falls back to the surface as precipitation. Some water that hits the ground runs off into streams and rivers and eventually to the sea.

As streams flow downhill towards the sea, they carry sediment with them. After rainfall, a stream contains more water and can carry more sediment.

The water cycle

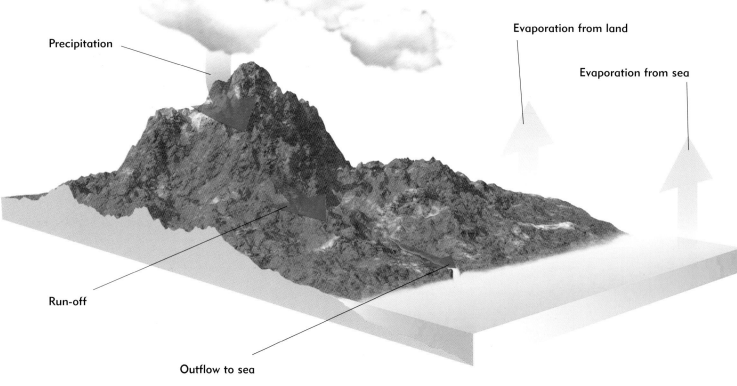

Precipitation

Evaporation from land

Evaporation from sea

Run-off

Outflow to sea

Sediment Transport

Rain hitting the ground washes soil into streams and rivers, where the soil forms sediment. Sediment is made up of tiny particles of clay, grains of sand, and pieces of rock of various sizes. Tiny particles are carried in the water; larger particles bump along the bottom. Mountain and upland streams and rivers flow quickly, and can move quite large rocks along. Further downstream, where the water slows down, larger particles of sediment settle on to the bed. The tiniest particles of sediment are carried to the sea, where they settle on to the sea-bed. The sediment from large rivers creates new land around the river mouth, called a **delta**.

As sediment moves along a river, it bumps against the bed and bank, wearing them away. This process is called erosion, and over millions of years it can create deep valleys.

Heating and Cooling

Rocks which are heated by the Sun during the day expand slightly because of the heat. At night, they cool down again, and contract (shrink). Over the years, this continuous expansion and contraction makes the rock crumble, creating sand, clay and soil.

Precipitation that falls on mountains runs into cracks in the rocks. In very cold weather, it freezes. Unlike most materials, which expand as they get warmer, ice expands slightly as it gets colder. Ice in a crack in a rock expands, widening the crack, and eventually breaking the rock apart.

 TEST FILE

ICE WEATHERING

You can easily see how, when water freezes, it can crack even the strongest rocks. Fill an old yogurt pot or plastic cup to the brim with cold water. Stand it carefully in a freezer. Now put a small piece of wood over the pot so that the water is covered. After a few hours, the water will have frozen, expanded, and pushed the wood upwards.

In windy places, small particles of weathered rock, such as grains of sand, are blown in the wind, scraping away at the rock.

WORLD WEATHER

The weather often seems random, but it does follow patterns. The most important is the pattern of winds over the Earth's surface. These winds are convection currents created because the Sun heats different parts of the surface by different amounts, which in turn heats the air in some areas more than others, creating wind patterns. These wind patterns help to create the type of weather each place has, which is called its climate (see page 32).

Cells of Wind

Because the Sun's rays are most concentrated at the Equator, parts of the Earth near the Equator and the air above is heated much more than parts of the Earth near the poles (see page 12). The air rises and spreads.

Air over the poles cools, sinks and spreads towards the Equator.

Between the Equator and the poles, this moving air sets up enormous circulating air currents, some of which are called Hadley cells after English scientist George Hadley (1686–1768), who first theorized that they existed.

How air circulates over the Earth's surface in cells.

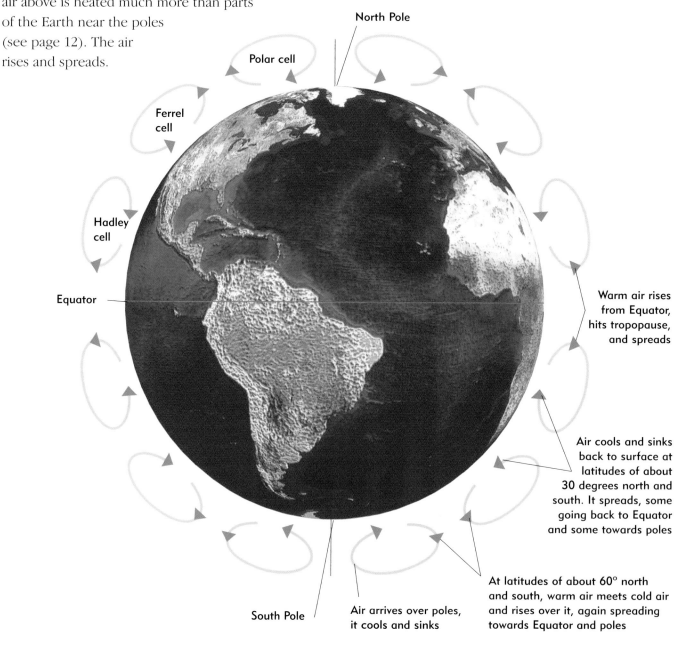

North Pole

Polar cell

Ferrel cell

Hadley cell

Equator

South Pole

Air arrives over poles, it cools and sinks

Warm air rises from Equator, hits tropopause, and spreads

Air cools and sinks back to surface at latitudes of about 30 degrees north and south. It spreads, some going back to Equator and some towards poles

At latitudes of about 60° north and south, warm air meets cold air and rises over it, again spreading towards Equator and poles

The Coriolis Effect

The circulating air in Hadley cells and other cells creates winds across the surface of the Earth which blow either towards the poles or towards the Equator. These winds do not blow directly to the north or to the south. Because the Earth spins on its axis, the winds curve across the surface, creating easterly and westerly winds. This effect is called the Coriolis effect after Gustave-Gaspard de Coriolis (1792–1843) who was first person to explain why winds blow to the east or west.

In the northern hemisphere, the Coriolis effect means that winds blowing towards the North Pole blow to the east and winds blowing towards the Equator blow to the west. The effects are reversed in the southern hemisphere.

HISTORY FILE

PREVAILING WINDS
• Trade winds are so called because traders in sailing ships made use of them to cross the oceans.
• North-easterly trade winds carried sailors from southern Europe to the Caribbean.
• The sailors returned by sailing north to pick up the westerlies (see Fact File).
• The 'Roaring Forties' are very strong westerlies which blow across the oceans of the southern hemisphere.
• Between these wind patterns are areas of calm, called the doldrums, which were feared by sailors.

FACT FILE

WINDS AND THEIR DIRECTION
• Wind cells combined with the Coriolis effect create winds which blow in the same direction most of the time.
• 'Trade winds' blow towards the Equator from the north east in the northern hemisphere and from the south east in the southern hemisphere.
• 'Westerlies' blow towards the poles from the south west in the northern hemisphere and from the north west in the southern hemisphere.
• 'Polar easterlies' blow away from the poles in both hemispheres.

Long-distance balloon pilots make use of high-level winds called jet streams that blow around the Earth.

LOWS AND HIGHS

The circulation of winds around the Earth (see page 26) creates bodies of air which have different temperatures and humidities. These are called air masses. Where two air masses meet, the boundary between them is called a front.

At latitudes of about 60° north and 60° south, approximately two-thirds of the way from the Equator to the poles (for example, in northern Europe, the northern USA and southern South America), two air masses meet. Cold, dry air moving away from the poles meets warmer, more humid air moving away from the tropics. The two air masses fight for space, creating swirling masses of air called weather systems.

Lows

Low-pressure systems or depressions, often just called 'lows', are weather systems in which the air swirls around a central area of low pressure. They start life at the boundary between cold, dry polar air and warm, moist tropical air, when the warm air rises over the top of the cold air, creating a region of low pressure. Cold air is drawn under the warm air and two moving fronts are now formed. On one front, called a cold front, cold air moves forwards under warm air ahead of it. On the other front, called a warm front, warm air rises over cold air ahead of it. These fronts begin to move around each other, forming a circulating weather system. Eventually the cold front catches up the warm front, forming a new type of front called an occluded front.

Because of the Coriolis effect, a low-pressure system rotates anti-clockwise in the northern hemisphere and clockwise in the southern hemisphere. The weather system moves along, spinning as it goes, creating winds. As the fronts in the system move over a place on the Earth's surface, the place experiences changes in weather.

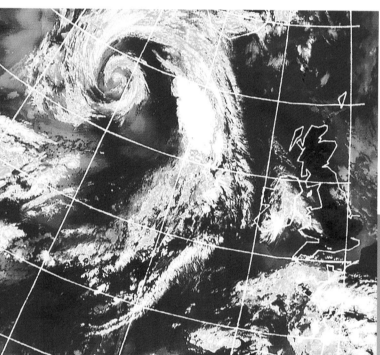

The swirl of a low-pressure system over the Atlantic Ocean

Cross-section through a warm front

Warm front

Warm air mass

High clouds arrive hours before front itself

Movement of mass of warm air

Stratus clouds bring rain or snow

Warm front

Warm air mass rises above mass of cold air in front of it

Cold air mass

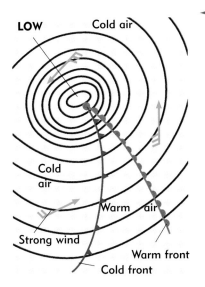

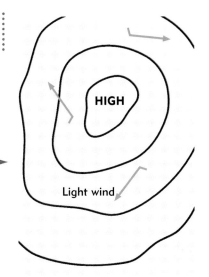

In a low pressure system, air moves inwards in an anticlockwise direction. Warm and cold air meet to create fronts; often accompanied by strong winds and rainfall.

In a high pressure system, air moves outward and in a clockwise direction. There are usually clear skies and light winds.

Highs

Areas of high pressure, also called anticyclones, or just 'highs', happen when air that has cooled sinks back to the Earth's surface. There are no fronts in a high, and highs spin more slowly than lows. Highs generally bring settled weather with clear skies and light winds. They are common around latitudes of 30° north and south, about one-third of the distance from the Equator to the poles.

TEST FILE

FINDING THE LOW
Find a weather map which shows where lows and highs will be today. If there is a low near where you live, go outside and stand so that the wind is blowing into your back. If you are in the northern hemisphere, a low pressure will be to your left. If you are in the southern hemisphere, a low pressure will be to your right. Check your findings against the weather map.

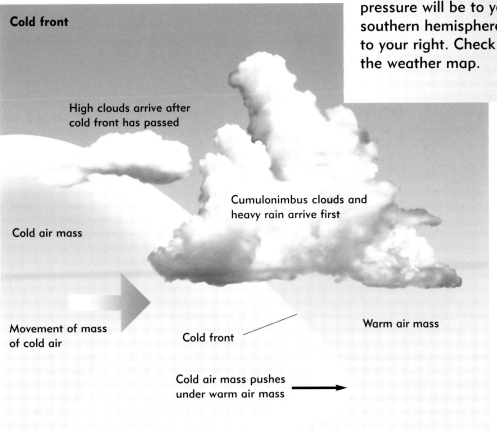

Cross-section through a cold front

29

WEATHER CYCLES

The weather always repeats itself over certain periods of time. We are all used to a yearly cycle of weather, where the weather is similar at the same time each year. This happens as the Earth makes its orbit around the Sun. There is often a daily cycle of weather, too, as the Earth spins on its axis and places warm up and cool down as the day goes by. The type and pattern of weather that a place experiences is called its climate (see page 32).

Daily Weather

At each place on Earth every day, the Sun rises, heats the surface and then sets, allowing the surface to cool again. The greatest heating happens at midday, when the Sun is at its highest in the sky. This heating and cooling sets up a daily cycle of weather.

For example, on a calm day, heating causes thermals to form, which create clouds in the late morning and afternoon. These may lead to showers which die away as the temperature cools in the evening. As the ground cools, dew, frost or fog may form. On the coast, sea breezes are set up (see page 20).

FACT FILE

ANIMALS IN WINTER
• In temperate climates with cold winters, some animals, such as squirrels and bears, go into hibernation for several months to save energy. Their body temperature drops, and their body functions slow down.
• Some animals migrate to warmer places in winter. For example, geese that spend summer in the Arctic fly to North America and Europe in winter to find food.
• Many animals grow a thicker coat in the autumn which gives them extra insulation against the cold in winter. They lose the coat again in spring.
• Animals such as the Arctic fox and Arctic hare grow a white winter coat for camouflage in the snowy landscape.

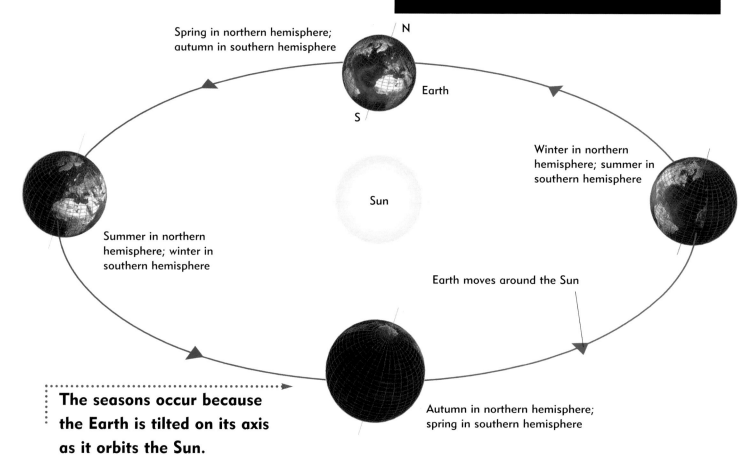

Spring in northern hemisphere; autumn in southern hemisphere

N

Earth

S

Winter in northern hemisphere; summer in southern hemisphere

Sun

Summer in northern hemisphere; winter in southern hemisphere

Earth moves around the Sun

Autumn in northern hemisphere; spring in southern hemisphere

The seasons occur because the Earth is tilted on its axis as it orbits the Sun.

The Seasons

Many areas of the world have distinct seasons which are repeated each year. In each season, the area experiences different types of weather. Seasons happen because the Earth's axis is tilted to one side, meaning that some parts of the surface are heated more at one time of the year (the summer) than another (the winter).

Areas in the middle and high latitudes experience four different seasons – spring, summer, autumn and winter. It's not only the weather that changes in each season. Plants and animals also change, going through different parts of their life cycles. For example, many species of trees shed their leaves in autumn and grow new ones in spring, and some birds migrate to warmer areas in winter.

In the tropics there are generally two seasons, a dry season and a rainy season, but the temperature stays almost the same all year round. Some places have a monsoon season, where seasonal winds create a few months of very heavy rains each year.

As the seasons change, they bring about changes in plants and animals. When autumn replaces summer, many trees change colour as their leaves die and fall to the ground.

FUTURE FILE

EL NIÑO

Warm and cool ocean currents have a huge effect on the weather because air masses move across them. These currents have patterns, too, with the most famous being the El Niño pattern of events. These occur every four to seven years, when warm water flows into the eastern Pacific Ocean. An El Niño event creates stormy weather on western coasts of the Americas, and is also responsible for droughts in Australia and wet and mild winters in Europe. Meteorologists are studying how the ocean currents and global weather are linked.

CLIMATES

The climate of a place is the sort of weather it has – not the weather each day, but its general pattern over a year. Climate depends on a huge variety of factors, but most important are latitude, altitude, the prevailing winds (the direction from which the wind blows most of the time), and the closeness of seas, oceans and mountains. There is evidence that climates are gradually changing (see page 42).

Because so many factors affect climate, places quite close together can have slightly different climates. For example, two places on opposite sides of a mountain can have quite different climates. This means that there are hundreds of different climates throughout the world, but meteorologists try to classify climates to give an idea of the weather that can be expected in an area. The name of the climate gives an idea of how the rainfall and temperature change as the year goes by. Areas which have different climates are called climate zones.

Lush, dense forests grow in the warm, wet tropics.

Graph of temperature (shown by the red line) and rainfall (coloured bars) in a tropical climate.

FACT FILE

CLIMATE ZONES
Polar: Long, very cold winters with high snowfall; short, cool summers.
Temperate: Some rain all year round; warm summers and cold winters, with some snow; winters longer and more severe towards the North and South poles.
Mediterranean: A coastal climate; hot and dry in summer; cool and wet in winter.
Dry: Very low rainfall all year round; hot summers and cool winters; hot days and cold nights.
Tropical: Hot and humid all year round; high rainfall with a short dry season.
Subtropical: Slightly cooler in winter than summer; wet and dry seasons; some areas have rainy seasons called monsoons.

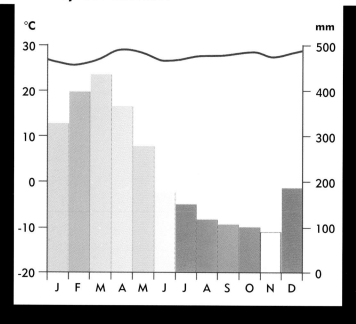

Coastal: Local climate around coast; less extreme temperature range than inland.
Mountain: Lower temperatures than surrounding areas; higher precipitation.

Examples of Climates

Most of northern Europe and the northern USA have a temperate climate. 'Temperate' means that the summers are warm rather than hot, and the winters are cold, perhaps with some snow. There is some rainfall all year round, and normally four distinct seasons.

Most places on and near the Equator have a tropical climate. 'Tropical' means that it is hot and humid, day and night, all year round, with high rainfall except for a short dry season.

Micro Climates

Geographical features such as seas, oceans, hills and mountains, and ocean currents, all have an effect on the climate of a place. Climates in small areas created by geographical features are called micro climates.

For example, places in mountains are normally colder than places on the **plains**, with more rain, snow and wind. Places in the lee of mountains (on the other side of the mountains to the prevailing winds) are often drier because the clouds drop their rain in the mountains.

Mt Kilimanjaro in Tanzania, Africa is much cooler than the sun-baked plains that surround it.

Meadows and deciduous trees are common in temperate climates.

Graph of temperature (shown by the red line) and rainfall (coloured bars) in a temperate climate.

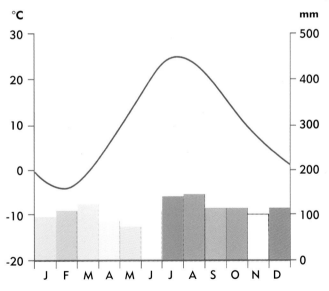

Along coasts, the sea and sea breezes tend to cut out the extremes of weather, such as snow, frost and very high temperatures. So a coastal climate tends to be cooler in summer and warmer in winter than places inland.

Cities also have their own micro climates, which are normally a few degrees warmer than the surrounding countryside.

STORMY WEATHER

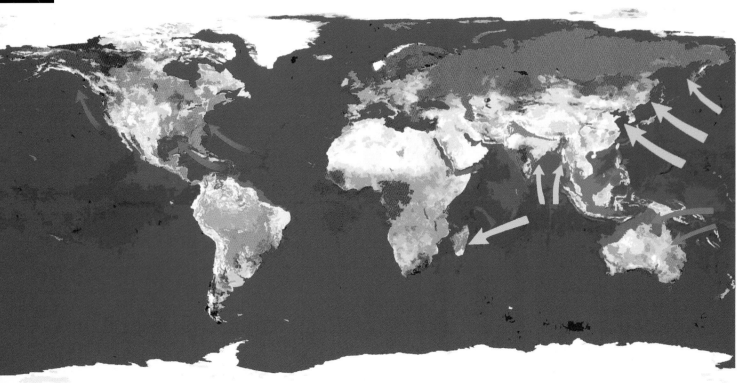

Certain combinations of temperature and humidity in some parts of the world can create damaging weather, with very heavy rain and extremely strong winds. Low-pressure systems can create winds up to storm force, with very heavy rain as fronts pass by. Slow-moving thunderstorms also create flash floods, but the strongest winds are caused by hurricanes and tornadoes.

Tropical storms are mostly found on the eastern shores of the Americas, Asia and Australia. They have different local names – hurricanes (shown in red), cyclones (green), typhoons (orange) and willy-willies (mauve).

Hurricanes

Hurricanes (called cyclones around Australia and the Indian Ocean, and typhoons in the Pacific and the China Sea) start life as a collection of thunderstorms over warm oceans, normally in the tropics. The storms develop into a low-pressure system hundreds of kilometres across, made up of thunderstorms circling a calm area called the eye. The system moves across the ocean away from the Equator, gathering strength as it goes. The winds blowing around it can average 250 kph, gusting to 300 kph.

A hurricane photographed by a weather satellite in space.

The aftermath of a tornado strike in Oklahoma, USA, in 1999.

FACT FILE

STORM FEATURES

• The severity of a tornado is measured on the Fujita Scale, which runs from F0 (winds up to 117 kph with 'light' damage) to F5 (winds of more than 418 kph with 'incredible' damage).

• The worst single tornado in history was the Tri-State Tornado which killed 695 people in the USA in 1925.

• Each new hurricane, typhoon or cyclone is given a name. New names are chosen alphabetically and are alternately female and male.

• The severity of a hurricane is measured on the Saffir-Simpson scale, which runs from category 1 (winds up to 152 kph with 'minimal damage') to category 5 (winds of more than 248 kph with 'catastrophic damage').

• The worst recorded storm of all time was a cyclone that hit Bangladesh in 1970, sweeping waves across the low-lying land at the delta, and drowning up to 500,000 people.

At sea, the strong winds whip up huge waves, and the low pressure sucks up the surface, creating a storm surge. The waves are a hazard to shipping, but most damage is done when a hurricane hits land, when the winds destroy buildings, the storm surge creates coastal flooding and the heavy rains create flooding inland, often with dangerous mud slides. Once inland, the hurricane subsides because it is deprived of the warm ocean from which it gets its energy.

Tornadoes

A tornado is a rapidly spinning column of air called a vortex which reaches down to the ground from a huge thundercloud. Inside the vortex, winds can reach nearly 500 kph. These incredibly strong winds rip buildings apart. A typical tornado is about 100 m across and moves slowly, tearing apart any buildings in its path. The vortex sucks up dust and other material from the ground, dropping it when the tornado subsides, up to an hour after it has begun. The Mid-West of the USA, known as Tornado Alley, is the area the of world most prone to tornadoes, but small ones can occur almost anywhere. Waterspouts, which move across water, are similar to tornadoes.

RECORDING THE WEATHER

Every day, at thousands of weather stations all over the world, people and machines take measurements and make observations of the atmosphere and the weather (temperature, pressure, wind speed and direction, humidity, rainfall, sunshine and so on). These are used not only to try to forecast what is likely to happen to the weather over the following few days (see page 38), but also to build up comprehensive weather records over the years.

Weather records have several uses. They help meteorologists to identify patterns of weather, which are useful in forecasting. They can also show up any changes in climate over the years (see page 42). Daily weather records are used to calculate monthly and yearly averages, which show weather patterns at a glance.

Most nations have an official national weather service which collects and stores weather records, normally on their computers. This ensures that records are recorded daily and are easy to access. The service is also responsible for weather forecasting.

Weather Stations

A typical small weather station contains a range of weather-measuring instruments. These are normally a barometer (to measure air pressure), and a thermometer (to measure air temperature), a maximum and minimum thermometer, a hygrometer or wet-bulb thermometer (to measure humidity), a rain gauge, and an anemometer (to measure wind speed) and a wind vane (to measure wind direction).

All the instruments except the rain gauge, anemometer and wind vane are kept inside a slatted wooden box, which protects them from direct sunlight but allows fresh air in. Readings are taken once or twice a day, always at the same time.

HISTORY FILE

EARLY WEATHER RECORDS
European scientists began building weather-measuring instruments and making recordings with them in the fifteenth century. But recordings were made in only a few places and were not continuous from year to year. Proper organized recordings started in the eighteenth century, with scientific organizations such as the Royal Society in Britain and the Mannheim Society in Germany collecting recordings from around the world.

A small hilltop weather station in the Antarctic.

A sunshine recorder automatically records when the Sun is shining by using the Sun's rays to burn a paper strip.

Automatic Instruments

Larger weather stations include instruments which record measurements throughout the day and night, either on paper or electronically. Automatic weather stations have electronic instruments connected via telephone lines or satellite links to weather centres.

Weather observations are also made from satellites orbiting the Earth. This is called remote sensing. These can take photographs of clouds, which shows how weather systems are moving, and are especially important in tracking storms. Satellites can also measure air temperatures, and sea and ground temperatures. Weather radars on the ground can spot precipitation tens of kilometres away, and so can help to give warnings of heavy rain, hail or snow.

 FACT FILE

WEATHER ON THE INTERNET
The Internet is a valuable tool for both professional and amateur meteorologists. It is used by meteorological organizations for collecting weather data and for publishing weather reports and forecasts. If you have access to the Web, you can see up-to-date satellite photographs and even get weather readings and photographs from some weather stations.

This weather balloon carries a small package of electronic instruments called a radiosonde which sends information about the atmosphere back to the ground.

FORECASTING

For most people, knowing what the weather is going to be like over the following few hours or days is useful so that they can plan their days and what clothes to wear. For others, such as pilots and sailors, an accurate forecast is essential. Forecasts of severe weather, such as high winds, heavy rain or thick fog, are important for everybody.

Forecasters use current measurements and observations, and weather records, to try to predict what will happen to the weather next. Forecasting for a few hours in the future is not too difficult, but long-range forecasts are more difficult because weather is very unpredictable.

Weather forecasting is normally the job of the national weather service of a country, but weather services also work together and share information. The World Meteorological Organization, which is part of the United Nations, collects data from all over the world and creates global weather forecasts.

Making a Forecast

Forecasters use data from weather stations, together with images from satellites, to draw up a picture of what is happening in the atmosphere. This huge amount of information is fed into dedicated computers programmed to model the atmosphere and how it will change over the following few hours or days. An experienced forecaster is still required to interpret the results and decide where, for example, it is likely to rain or be foggy.

FACT FILE

FORECASTING WITH NATURE
• The saying 'Red sky at night, shepherd's delight, red sky in the morning, shepherd's warning' is normally right as red sky at night means that dry air is on the way.
• Many flowers close up their petals just before rain falls to protect their pollen. They react to the humid air.
• Seaweed can test humidity – in humid weather it takes in water vapour from the air and becomes soft. Fircones close up when the air is humid.
• Bees are said to forecast bad weather by not flying, probably because bees like flying on warm, dry, calm days.
• The storm petrel (a large seabird) is named because sailors believe that it flies close to the shore before a big storm arrives.
• Cows lie down before rain, probably because they can sense changes in humidity.

Weather Maps

The weather, whether it is the weather that is happening now, or a forecast of what might be happening in future, is shown on a weather map. This is series of symbols on top of a map of the Earth's surface which shows air pressures, winds, rain, cloud cover, and so on. Meteorologists use standard international symbols.

Meteorologists use computers to process data from weather stations and to predict how the weather will change.

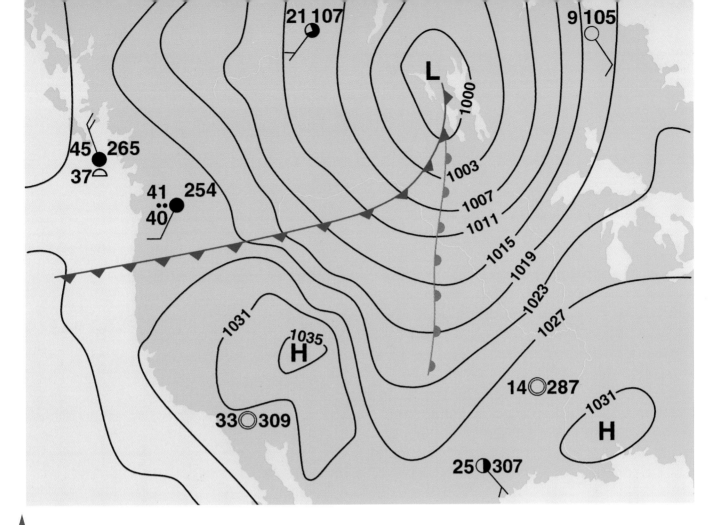

A type of weather map called a synoptic chart, which shows the weather at a particular point in time. The symbols on the map show the conditions at a particular weather station.

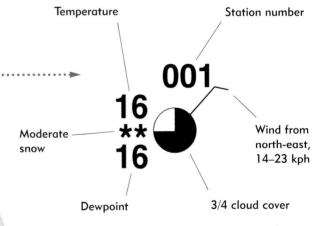

Temperature

Station number

001

16

** ** **

16

Moderate snow

Dewpoint

Wind from north-east, 14–23 kph

3/4 cloud cover

FUTURE FILE

ACCURACY OF FORECASTS

The accuracy of forecasting is likely to keep increasing as computers become more powerful and meteorologists continue to learn about the complex workings of the atmosphere and so can create better computer models. But it may never be possible to forecast more than about ten days ahead because of the incredibly complex way in which the atmosphere behaves. In theory, even the tiniest change, such as the breeze created as you breathe, could trigger off a storm weeks later on the other side of the world!

Communicating a Forecast

Weather maps used by meteorologists are quite complex and difficult for most people to understand. When forecasters are preparing a forecast for the general public, for example for a newspaper or for television, they use simplified maps. Specialist forecasts for pilots, sailors and mountaineers normally give more detail. These are often available over the telephone, by fax, or on the Internet.

DESIGNING FOR WEATHER

Many areas of the world are prone to very high or very low temperatures, high humidity, strong winds or heavy rain. People who live in these areas have developed ways of dealing with these extremes of weather, such as wearing particular clothes. Advanced warnings are more important in these areas, too, so that people can stay indoors or be evacuated.

Animals and plants have evolved ways of dealing with extremes of weather, too, so that there are species which can survive in almost all the world's climates.

Clothing and Temperature

Your body always tries to maintain a constant temperature. If your body gets too warm, you sweat. The sweat evaporates from your skin, which cools you down. If you get too cold, hairs on your skin stand on end, trying to give you extra insulation, and you might shiver, which creates heat inside your muscles.

Insulated clothing helps keep people warm in cold climates (left). Loose, light-coloured clothes allow cool air to reach the body and keep out the Sun in hot climates (right).

FACT FILE

EXTREME CLIMATE ADAPTATION
Below are some examples of how plants and animals have adapted to survive in extreme climates.

• Some plants that grow in dry climates reduce water loss by having no leaves. They store water in their fleshy stems. Other plants grow only after the annual rains have arrived.
• Coniferous trees, which grow in cold temperate climates, have needle-like leaves which helps to prevent them freezing. Many are also good at shedding snow because their branches often grow downwards and snow slides off them.
• Camels have adapted to desert life by being able to drink more than a hundred litres of water in one go and then nothing for days on end.
• Some insects survive in polar climates by making natural antifreeze that prevents the water in their bodies from freezing.

Engineers must take into account the weather records when designing structures. For example, a bridge must withstand winds that might only come along once every hundred years.

In hot, humid weather, the Sun's rays heat you up, and sweating does not work well because evaporation is slow in the humid air. In these conditions, loose-fitting, light-coloured clothing is best. The light colours reflect the Sun's rays, and cool air can circulate near the skin, carrying away heat and helping evaporation.

In very cold temperatures, your body loses heat very quickly to the air. Wearing insulating clothing reduces the movement of heat by trapping tiny pockets of air in its fibres. But it only works if it stays dry, so a waterproof outer layer is important in wet weather.

Wind blowing across your skin helps to carry heat away from your body, making the air feel colder. This effect is called wind chill. This is useful for keeping you cool in hot weather, but a nuisance in cold weather, when windproof clothing is vital.

Buildings

Buildings are also designed to cope with extremes of weather, both to create a comfortable climate for the occupants and so that they stay standing.

In hot climates, stone or concrete houses are painted white to reflect the Sun's rays. Most office buildings have air conditioning systems which maintain the temperature and humidity of the air at a comfortable level. In cold climates, homes are insulated to prevent heat loss. In snowy climates, they may have sloping roofs to shed heavy snowfalls.

These buildings in Greece are painted white to reflect the Sun's rays, which helps to keep them cool inside.

CHANGING WEATHER

You have probably heard about 'global warming'. It means that the average temperature of the air in the lower atmosphere, where the weather happens, is increasing very slowly. In the past hundred years, it has risen by about 0.5 °C, but some scientists predict that it will rise more quickly in the next few decades.

Meteorologists are not yet sure whether this increase in temperature is part of a natural cycle or is caused by human activities. Neither are they sure whether events such as severe droughts and storms are the results of global warming.

Historical Climates

What is certain is that the temperature has fluctuated a great deal since the Earth was formed about 4,600 million years ago. Scientists know this, for example, from studying rocks and fossils of the different species of animals and plants from different parts of the world, and by studying layers of ice at the poles.

For most of the last 200 million years, the average temperature was several degrees warmer than it is today, so that animals and plants could live at the now-freezing poles. About 65 million years ago, the Earth began to cool, and there were periods of cold temperatures, called ice ages, when glaciers formed in mountains and thick ice sheets stretched for many thousands of kilometres from the poles.

Deforestation of the world's rain forests releases huge amounts of the greenhouse gas carbon dioxide into the atmosphere.

Activities that Change Climate

Environmentalists claim that human activities such as burning fossil fuels and cutting down rain forests are responsible for global warming. Some scientists agree; others are not convinced that there is enough evidence.

The main reason for current global warming may be the greenhouse effect. This is the process by which the Sun's heat is trapped by some of the gases in the atmosphere. These gases are called the greenhouse gases, and are mainly carbon dioxide, ozone and water vapour.

This graph shows how the average world air temperature has changed over the last 10,000 years.

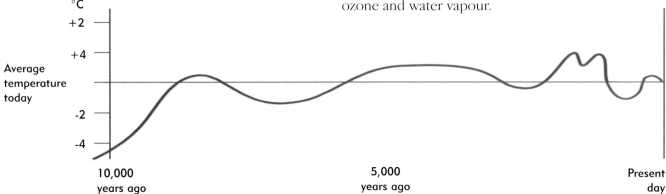

°C	
+2	
+4	
Average temperature today	
-2	
-4	

10,000 years ago	5,000 years ago	Present day

Ice cores are a good record of atmospheric change up to 100,000 years ago. Air bubbles in the ice show how the gases in the air have changed, too.

 FUTURE FILE

MELTING POLAR ICE CAPS
One of the major effects of global warming would be that the polar ice caps would begin to melt. There is already evidence that this is beginning to happen. The water released would flow into the oceans, making them deeper, and flooding low-lying islands and coastal areas. If all the ice in Greenland melted, sea levels would rise more than 7 m world-wide. If all the polar ice melted, levels would rise by an incredible 65 m.

FACT FILE

ICE AGES
• The most recent ice age happened about 18,000 years ago. The northern USA, northern Europe, Argentina and New Zealand were covered with ice up to 3 km thick.
• When the ice melted, sea levels rose, covering low-lying land and leaving the coasts we know today.
• The 'Little Ice Age' was a era of extremely cold winters which lasted from about 1450 to about 1850.
• Disastrous events such as meteor collisions and volcanic eruptions throw dust into air, cutting out sunlight and creating years of cold temperatures. It's estimated that 99 per cent of all the species that have ever evolved (including the dinosaurs) have been wiped out by these events.

Without the greenhouse effect, the Earth would be too cold for life, but burning fossil fuels creates extra greenhouse gases, meaning more energy is trapped than before, with a resulting increase in air temperature.

In the last decade there have been several international climate conferences at which countries have agreed to try to reduce the production of greenhouse gases by measures such as reducing fuel consumption and using more renewable energy. This is not easy, and is more difficult in developing industrial economies, where these measures would be too expensive and cost valuable jobs.

GLOSSARY AND FURTHER INFO

Altitude How far a place is above mean sea level (the average level of the sea taking tides into account), measured in metres or feet.

Convection The process of heat moving from one place to another, carried by air or water making a convection current.

Delta An area of low-lying land at the mouth of a river, created by sediment (mud, silt, sand, etc.) carried down the river.

Density The amount of a substance that fits into a certain space, measured in kilograms per cubic metre.

Dewpoint The temperature at which water vapour in the air becomes saturated and dew begins to form.

Equator An imaginary line drawn around the Earth halfway between the North and South poles.

Evaporation The process of water molecules (or molecules of any other liquid) escaping from the surface of a body of water to create water vapour in the air above.

Humidity The amount of moisture, or water vapour, in the air.

Latitude The distance of a place on the Earth's surface from the Equator, measured in degrees (the Equator is at zero degrees and the poles are at 90°).

Molecules The smallest natural particles of a substance. For example, water molecules are made up of hydrogen and oxygen atoms.

Plains Broad, level areas of land, such as the prairies of North America.

Pollutants Substances that contaminate or damage the environment.

Precipitation The name for water vapour that condenses in the atmosphere. Rain, snow, hail, and dew are all forms of precipitation.

Radiation The movement of energy from one place to another in the form of rays. Light, infra-red light, X-rays and radio waves are all examples of radiation.

Relative humidity A measure of the amount of water vapour in the air. It is expressed as a percentage of the amount of water vapour there would be if the air contained as much as it could hold at that temperature.

Saturated When air contains as much water vapour as it can hold at a certain temperature. (Warm air can hold more water vapour than cool air.)

Sediment Material that has been deposited by a river, a glacier or ice sheet, or the wind.

Thermals Rising columns of warm air.

Tropics The part of the Earth between the latitudes 23.5° north (the Tropic of Cancer) and 23.5° south (the Tropic of Capricorn).

ORGANIZATIONS TO CONTACT

The Meteorological Office
Bracknell, Berkshire RG12 1AA
The national weather service of the UK.

Friends of the Earth
26-28 Underwood Street, London N1 7JQ
An organization that campaigns world-wide to protect the environment.

Royal Meteorological Society
104 Oxford Road, Reading, Berks RG1 7LJ
An organization for weather experts and enthusiasts.

BOOKS TO READ

Eyewitness Weather by Brian Cosgrove (Dorling Kindersley, 1991)
Horrible Geography: Stormy Weather by Anita Ganeri (Scholastic Children's Books, 1999)
How the Weather Works by Michael Allaby (Dorling Kindersley, 1995)
Learn about Weather by Robin Kerrod (Lorenz Books, 1998)
Storms and Hurricanes by Kathy Gemmel (Usborne Publishing, 1995)
Weather Watch series: *Rain, Snow, Frost, Wind, Storms, Heatwave* (Watts Books)

WEB SITES

World Meteorological Organization
www.wmo.ch
Site of the international weather organization. Latest news on climate change.

National Oceanic and Atmospheric Administration
www.nws.noaa.gov
The national weather-forecasting service of the USA. Forecasts, downloadable maps and links.

The Meteorological Office
www.met-office.gov.uk
The national weather service of the UK. Forecasts, maps, links and general information.

The Tornado and Storm Research Organization
www.torro.org.uk
Information about the latest tornadoes and hurricanes.

INDEX

Cirrus
These are high, wispy clouds that are found 10–15 km above the ground. At this height, the temperature is below freezing, so cirrus clouds consist of ice.

Altostratus
This appears as grey or bluish layers of cloud through which the Sun may just be visible. It normally means that rain is on the way.

Nimbostratus
Raincloud which often appears as a grey layer that covers much of the sky and blots out the Sun.

Cumulus
These are heavy, heap-shaped clouds with flat bases. They look bright white in sunlight. Cumulus clouds may develop into cumulonimbus.

Stratus
This is a thick, grey, low cloud which often brings fog, drizzle or rain. It frequently covers high ground.

Cirrocumulus
These clouds, which look like ripples, are often seen after a low has passed. They may signal the arrival of fair weather.

Altocumulus
Layers of altocumulus cloud appear in groups or in lines. They often mean that there is unsettled weather on the way.

Cumulonimbus
These thunderclouds are tall and anvil shaped. They can start as low as 1,000 m above the ground and stretch up to over 10,000 m. They bring rain, hail, thunder and lightning.

CLOUD NAMES

The names given to different types of cloud come from Latin words. Most clouds have names that are a combination of two Latin words.

- Cirrus comes from a word meaning 'hair' or 'curl'.
- Cumulus means 'heap'.
- Stratus comes from *stratum*, meaning 'something that is spread out or laid down'.
- Nimbus means 'storm cloud'.
- The names of high-level clouds (above 5,000 m from the ground) often begin with the prefix 'cirro'.
- Mid-level cloud names (between 2,000 and 5,000 m) begin with 'alto'.
- Low-level clouds (below 2,000 m) do not begin with a prefix.